Praise for "Cooking with Lavender"

Cooking with Lavender will become as dog-eared and stained as the other culinary books in my kitchen, and lavender will take its place on my spice rack beside cumin, thyme, and coriander. — **readingnewmexico.com**

Praise for Smith's other cookbooks . . .

On Recipes for Romance:

"You'll have a great time whipping up romantic meals with this cookbook." —Ruth Glick, cookbook author, Columbia, MD

"Smith's recipe collection is full of inspiring dishes to create romantic meals." —Stamatios Palios, owner–chef, Stamo's Café, Bellevue, WA

"This is a fabulous cookbook for the romantic at heart." —Laura Baker, award-winning romantic suspense author, Albuquerque, NM

"Recipes for Romance. . . silken, sensuous, whip-it-up-in-a-minute recipes for great romantic meals." —Katy Korkos, proprietor, Katherine's Restaurant, White Rock, NM

"Even newlywed kitchen novices can prepare romantic meals together with Recipes for Romance. Guaranteed." —newlyweds John & Kirstin Loth, Columbus, OH

On Pumpkin Recipes:

"My wife and I bought your Pumpkin Recipes book a few weekends ago, and are delighted with it. Your recipes are simple and exquisite. Congratulations on an excellent job." —Ed Santiago, Los Alamos, NM

"Terrific recipes, even for the gluten-intolerant, thanks to the information in the introduction about how to modify the wheat-containing recipes to gluten-free ones." —Karen Smith, gluten intolerance expert, Ann Arbor, MI

". . . can help you lose weight. Pumpkin Recipes is full of good, healthy recipes to help you curb your appetite without a lot of calories." —Bette Johnson, R.N., Madison, SD

Cooking with Lavender

Suzanne T. Smith

Rio Grande Books

OBSESSION DU JOUR PRESS
Los Alamos, New Mexico

Cooking with Lavender
by Suzanne T. Smith

© 2008 by Suzanne T. Smith.
Published by Rio Grande Books in collaboration with Obsession du Jour Press

Printed in the United States of America.

Front cover photo courtesy the Rembe family, Los Poblanos Lavender Fields, Los Ranchos, NM
Design by Paul Rhetts, Los Ranchos, NM

Produced and published by:
Rio Grande Books
925 Salamanca NW
Los Ranchos, NM 87107-5647 USA
505-344-9382
E-mail: info@nmsantos.com

Obsession du Jour Press
185 Laguna
Los Alamos NM 87544-2603 USA
505-662-3744
E-mail: stsodj@aol.com

Library of Congress Cataloging-in-Publication Data

Smith, Suzanne T.
 Cooking with lavender / by Suzanne T. Smith.
   p. cm.
 Includes bibliographical references and index.
 ISBN-13: 978-1-890689-77-3 (pbk.)
 ISBN-10: 1-890689-77-7 (pbk.)
 1. Cookery (Lavender) 2. Lavenders--New Mexico. I. Title.
 TX819.L38S65 2008
 641.6--dc22
                              2008019109

For Ron, Emma, and Clancy

Acknowledgments

My special thanks go to Rosalie Carle, known in our area as "The Lavender Lady," who started me on this venture by suggesting that I should write a lavender cookbook. Rosalie produces a catalog through her company, *Rosalie of Santa Fe, Inc.*, offering sachets she fashions from locally grown lavender in a variety of creative designs reflecting the multicultural spirit of Santa Fe and New Mexico–the Land of Enchantment To order a copy of her catalog, contact her by phone at 505-424-0926, fax at 505-424-0928, or e-mail at RosalieSF@AOL.com.

I owe thanks to Joanna Gardner for her excellent marketing suggestions; to Mike Black at Black Studio for the photo for my bio; to Caryn Burtt at Random House for her help in the permission to use the front cover photo; to Dan Poynter at ParaPublishing for showing me how to write back cover copy; to Randy Murray at For The Love of Lavender for the interest and publicity he has generated for this book; and to Inez Ross at Ashley House for showing me how to sell books.

Many thanks also go to my friends and family for contributing the originals of some of these recipes, which I, of course, modified. And many thanks go as well to my critique group—Angie Chipera, D'Arcy Fowler, Joanna Gardner, Ron Smith, and Linda Wood—for their helpful comments throughout the development and editing stages of the book.

And finally, many thanks to Barbe Awalt and Paul Rhetts for their interest and encouragement for this book and their help in making it available to the public.

Table of Contents

About Lavender

Ah, lavender! The sturdy plants, the graceful blossoms, the spicy fragrance, the tangy taste of the flowers and the leaves—I love everything about this delightful herb. When I began to write this book, I discovered that many people with whom I spoke were familiar with lavender's uses in landscaping, aromatherapy, perfume, salves, and sachets, but few of them knew about cooking with this unique herb.

Lavender (*Lavandula* species) is a relative of mint and rosemary. It grows well in northern New Mexico where I live, and it pops up often in public and private gardens throughout the Southwest. With the western trend toward xeriscaping, lavender is a sought-after xeric plant whose uses are only beginning to be explored. Once established, lavender's drought tolerance makes it a garden favorite in arid climates.

Lavender through the Ages—A Brief History

Known in Biblical times as spikenard, lavender originated in the dry mountainous regions of southern Europe, the Middle East, and North Africa. Lavender was popular with the Greeks, Romans, Persians, and Carthaginians of old. From the Mediterranean, Roman legions, trades-men, and knights returning from the Crusades spread it northward and westward through Europe and eventually to the British Isles.

Lavender first came to the Americas more than four centuries ago. Brought into Mexico and then northward along the Rio Grande to northern New Mexico by the Spaniards, it was a significant part of the medicine chests of the Conquistadores. Today in Alcalde, a town in northern New Mexico, a study is underway by New Mexico State University to examine lavender's potential as a cash crop for the state.

Lavender's original name comes from the Latin word lavare, meaning "to wash." Ancient Greeks and Romans bathed in purifying lavender-scented water. From earliest times, healers burned lavender as incense to freshen sickrooms and cleanse hospitals.

Many tales about lavender have been handed down through time. The ancient Greeks wrapped sacrificial virgins in branches of lavender and laurel before burning them to appease their angry gods. Another ancient superstition maintained that asps made their nests in lavender bushes, which, some speculated, allowed herbalists to inflate prices for the fragrant herb because of the implicit dangers in gathering it.

In the Middle Ages, many people considered lavender to be an aphrodisiac, although at the same time, amusingly, others believed that a sprinkle of lavender water on the head would keep the wearer chaste. English washer-women used lavender in their wash and rinse

1

water, and hence were known as "lavenders." That same term was applied in medieval times to courtesans, light-skirts, and ladies of the night.

In Tudor times, lavender was used extensively in both cooking and medicine. Lavender also appeared in the geometric, hedge-bordered flower gardens known as Elizabethan knot gardens.

But lavender wasn't just for peasants and commoners. Several heads of state developed great fondness for lavender as well. Charles VI of France (1368-1422), also called Charles the Mad, used satin cushions and bed pillows stuffed with lavender. England's Queen Elizabeth I (1533-1603) especially liked lavender conserve, and she also enjoyed its flavor in savory foods. Napoleon Bonaparte (1769-1821) poured refreshing lavender water over his head and shoulders when he washed. Queen Victoria of England (1819-1901) kept her homes filled with the scent of lavender from bouquets and sachets.

Lavender was indispensable in Victorian times as an ingredient of the aromatic spirits of ammonia, used to revive Victorian ladies with "the vapors" or fainting spells. Up until World War I, lavender was used as a disinfectant for wounds. Even today in China, lavender is an ingredient in a cure-all medicinal oil called White Flower Oil.

Kabyle women in North Africa believe that lavender protects them from abuse by their husbands. In Tuscany, many mothers pin lavender sprigs to their children's clothing to protect the child from the evil eye. Some odder uses for lavender over the ages include embalming corpses and taming lions and tigers. Give the Lavender Crêpes Suzanne on page 29 a try to help you tame the wild beasts in your life.

Cooking with Lavender

Chefs throughout the ages have used the lemony-tasting flowers and bitterly pungent leaves of lavender in appetizers, salads, vinegars, jellies, sauces, main dishes, desserts, and beverages. You can use lavender in your own cooking to titillate the tongues and tickle the palates of your family and friends.

The sweet, lemony flavor of lavender blossoms pairs beautifully with seafood and poultry, baked goods, confections, and fruit dishes. What's more, lavender flowers have a natural affinity for oranges. For a real treat, crystallize some lavender blossoms to use as a garnish.

You probably know about using the robustly flavored, grayish-green leaves and stalks of the lavender plant principally for the strong fragrance of their essential oils. But did you know you can also use them with a light hand in cooking hearty dishes like soups, stews, beef, lamb, pork, poultry, and game? Lavender flowers, leaves, and stalks are used extensively in French, Mediterranean, and Middle Eastern cuisines, and moderately in the cuisine of England. The fresher the lavender, the milder its flavor and the more you can use in cooking.

Sources for Culinary Lavender

Take care that any lavender you use for cooking hasn't been sprayed with fragrance-enhancing oils or perfumes, pesticides, or any other substances hazardous to human health. When ordering lavender through the mail or on the Internet, be sure that the description includes the words "culinary lavender." Even better, track down a source of certified organic lavender. Culinary lavender appears in specialty stores, gourmet shops, herb stores, farmers' markets, and arts and crafts fairs.

If you search diligently, you probably can find some sources for culinary lavender in

2

your area. Meanwhile, here are some mail-order sources to get you started. If you want to visit any of the lavender growers, please call ahead to assure a visit is acceptable at that time.

Wildcat Lavender   1-505-438-1194
30 South Fork   wclavender@cybermesa.com
Santa Fe NM 87508
Culinary lavender, lavender grilling sticks, teas, skin and body products, and more

Matanzas Creek Winery   1-800-590-6464
6097 Bennett Valley Road   matcrkwine@aol.com
Santa Rosa CA 95404   www.matanzascreek.com
Culinary lavender, lavender food products

Growing Lavender

Unless you require huge quantities, the best way to obtain a good grade of culinary lavender is to grow and harvest your own. In addition to being sure the lavender is unsprayed, you'll have the pleasure of lavender's beauty and fragrance in your garden all summer long.

Lavender grows wild in southern France, Spain, Italy, Corsica, and Sicily, as well as in the rocky, chalky soils of other countries bordering the Mediterranean Sea. In these countries, lavender flowers and leaves are the signature ingredient of herbes de Provence, a mixture of indigenous aromatic herbs that also includes various combinations of the flowers and leaves of the more common basil, bay, marjoram, rosemary, savory, and thyme. Avoid blends that don't include lavender— they aren't true representations of herbes de Provence.

The climate here in the higher elevations of northern New Mexico is ideal for growing lavender, where many municipalities—including Los Alamos—display lavender as landscaping in public places. Most lavender varieties thrive at these higher altitudes in dry, light, gravelly, or stony soil. Give lavender full sun, well-drained soil, and protection from the wind, and the plants will reward you with blossoms and fragrance. Drier growing conditions encourage the development of lavender's aromatic oils, although drought conditions discourage flowering.

Varieties of Lavender for Culinary Purposes

More than 200 varieties of lavender are known worldwide. At least 28 varieties of perennial lavender, cold-hardy to 0°– 15° Fahrenheit, are under cultivation in climate Zones 4–8. All are more or less suitable for culinary purposes, having lemony-tasting flowers with varying degrees of sweetness or bitterness and leaves with a pungent tang similar to rosemary. A general-purpose gardening book or your county agricultural extension agent can provide information about your local climate zone.

Lavender connoisseurs consider *Lavandula angustifolia*—English lavender—to be the best variety for cooking because the flowers have a sweet, lemony flavor and the leaves, while bitter, do not have the heavy camphor characteristic exhibited by other lavender species. Some popular varieties of *L. angustifolia* are:

✿ 'Hidcote,' 12 inches tall with deep purple blossoms;
✿ 'Munstead,' best suited for cold climates, 12–18 inches tall, produces deep lavender flowers several weeks earlier than other varieties;
✿ 'Alba' with its pretty white flowers;

3

- ❀ 'Compacta,' only 10 inches tall and 12 inches in spread;
- ❀ 'Jean Davis,' 18 inches tall with pink flowers;
- ❀ 'Twickle Pink,' 24–25 inches tall with large spikes of very fragrant flowers;
- ❀ 'Nana,' a dwarfed and compact variety;
- ❀ 'Triphylla,' which has small leaflets at the base of the flowers;
- ❀ 'Rosea;' with its rosy pink blossoms; and
- ❀ *L. angustifolia* subsp. *angustifolia*, which has small stalks and an early blooming habit.

All these varieties all do well in our sunny northern New Mexico climate, and all are cold-hardy to about 0% F, although some winter protection is necessary because of drying winds.

Other English lavenders (*L. vera, L. officianalis, L. delphinensis,* and *L. spica*) have more bitter leaves that should be used sparingly so as not to overwhelm other flavors. The blossoms, however, add a lemony piquancy to sweets, salads, and beverages.

French lavender (*L. dentata*), reaching 24–36 inches in height, is considered a tender perennial, hardy to only 15° F. Its dark lavender flowers above inch-long, grey-green, toothed leaves bloom year-round in mild climates; it should winter indoors in cold climates. The fernlike leaves of French lavender are slightly less bitter than those of English lavender. Wild French lavender, the variety known to the ancients, tastes somewhat like balsam and rosemary.

Spanish lavenders (*L. stoechas,* with its purple bracts, and L. latifolia, usually called spike lavender) are tender perennials hardy to 0° F with wind and winter protection. They have an almost rosemary-like fragrance. Like French lavender, they, too, usually do better wintered indoors in cold climates. Spanish lavender leaves, particularly those of L. stoechas, have more of a camphor characteristic than other varieties that goes well with hearty meats and game dishes. In addition, the oil from *L. latifolia* is used in making lacquers and varnishes.

Harvesting and Storing Lavender

Harvest lavender at midday when oils are the most concentrated. Pick the stalks when the flowers show color but are not fully open.

To dry lavender, tie stalks together in bundles, then tie a brown paper bag around each bundle to keep out dust and insects. Hang the bundles in a warm, dry place until the stalks are completely dry. You can also use a food dehydrator if you have one, but Blose and Cusick (see *Bibliography*) recommend against drying lavender in a microwave.

Lavender blossoms and stems must be thoroughly dry to prevent rot and mold in storage. Store thoroughly dried lavender flowers and leaves in lidded glass jars or tins.

Lavender Resources in New Mexico

The first stop to find out about lavender is to go to local lavender festivals. Lavender in the Village takes place mid-July in Los Ranchos, just north of Albuquerque on Rio Grande Boulevard. Activities include vendors, visits to the lavender fields of Los Poblanos, and lavender products galore including foods. The last part of July is the Lavender and Herb Fair at El Rancho de Las Golondrinas in Santa Fe. This popular event allows visitors to visit herb fields, sample, and make lavender wands. Both events have websites for dates and times.

New Mexico farms have plenty of lavender for every use. Los Poblanos Lavender Fields in Los Ranchos, Lavender Spring Ranch in Lincoln County, Purple Adobe Lavender

Farm in Rio Arriba County, Enchanted Lavender in Albuquerque, Frolicking Deer Lavender Farm in Datil, and Black Pearl in Placitas offer products and lots of lavender. Call first to make sure they are open and have what you need. All are on the web.

The best places to find lavender may be at local farmers markets. The Los Alamos Farmers Market, Santa Fe Farmers Market, and Los Ranchos Growers Market have herb vendors, foods, and live plants to get you started.

Other Uses for Lavender

As a fragrant herb, lavender is used in sachets and bath preparations, to freshen sick-rooms, and as an ingredient in smelling salts. Lavender leaves repel moths and other insects, so use them in closets, drawers, and pet bedding. Some varieties of snuff include dried lavender as a flavor enhancement.

Lavender can expel gas from the rumbling digestive systems of the stomach and intestines. It can reduce or even stifle spasms, and it has both antiseptic and stimulant powers. In France and Spain, lavender compresses are used to treat bruises and bites. In herbal medicine, lavender has been used with varying efficacy as a medicine for quieting coughs, hysteria, nervous palpitations, hoarseness, palsy, toothaches, sore joints, apoplexy, and colic.

When you're stressed out, make a lavender infusion as a calming sedative. Pour a pint of boiling water over a teaspoon of lavender flowers. Steep the lavender for 15-20 minutes, strain the liquid into a mug, and sip your troubles away.

Or try this: two drops of lavender oil mixed with a cup of bland vegetable oil soothes skin irritation, eczema, and psoriasis. A few drops of the same mixture in a hot bath will lessen the pain of neuralgia or sore feet and, as a bonus, will leave you smelling irresistible.

Head to your local bookstore or visit your public library, and go on your own quest for lavender lore. Check out the many other uses of lavender in the books listed in my book's bibliography or in other books you may find, and see what else you can discover for your own cooking.

Better yet, give lavender a try in your garden and your kitchen. You'll have fun growing your own lavender for cooking, you'll dazzle friends and family with a new taste sensation, and you'll delight yourself in discovering the versatility of this enchanting herb!

Let me know how you like these recipes when you begin your own adventures in *Cooking with Lavender*.

Suzanne T. Smith
stsodj@aol.com
Los Alamos, New Mexico, USA

Lavender Recipes

Red Raspberry—Lavender Soup

This cold summer soup is my own creation. It's refreshing served either as a soup course or as a dessert. If you serve it as a dessert, you might also pass a platter of Lavender Mini-Meringues (see page 32) as an accompaniment. Serves 6.

4 cups fresh red raspberries
½ cup Chambord, other raspberry liqueur, or raspberry juice
¼ cup Grand Marnier, other orange liqueur, or orange juice
½ cup red zinfandel wine or non-alcoholic red wine
1½ cups half-and-half
1 tablespoon grated orange rind
2 tablespoons freshly squeezed orange juice
1 tablespoon dried lavender flowers
pinch ground allspice
pinch cayenne pepper
6 tablespoons sour cream or plain yogurt
18 fresh red raspberries for garnish
6 sprigs of lavender or mint for garnish

Combine 4 cups raspberries, Chambord, Grand Marnier, red zinfandel wine, half-and-half, grated lemon rind, lemon juice, lavender flowers, allspice, and cayenne pepper in a blender or food processor until smooth. Pour into a glass bowl or lidded container. Chill in refrigerator at least two hours.

To serve, ladle into pretty glass bowls and, for each serving, float a tablespoon of sour cream and 3 raspberries; top sour cream with a sprig of lavender or mint for garnish.

Wild Mushroom—
Barley Soup with Lavender

This is a scrumptious soup for a snowy day in winter or a rainy spring day. Perhaps you might like to serve it at an aprés ski party, along with a salad of mixed winter greens and crusty French bread. Don't forget the hot mulled wine or cider! Serves 8.

6 cups assorted fresh wild mushrooms (button, cèpes or porcini, shiitake, straw, wood-ear, chanterelle, trompette, morel, matsutake, truffle, Portobello, or oyster—whatever is available), stemmed and sliced; reserve 16 slices for garnish
4 tablespoons extra-virgin olive oil, peanut oil, or butter, divided
2 medium onions, finely chopped
2 celery ribs, finely chopped
2 large carrots, finely chopped
4 scallions, tops included, thinly sliced
⅔ cup unbleached all-purpose flour
4 cups beef broth
6 tablespoons barley
2 bay leaves
2 teaspoons dried whole-leaf thyme, or 4 teaspoons fresh thyme
2 teaspoons dried lavender blossoms and stems, or 4 teaspoons fresh lavender
½ teaspoon freshly ground black pepper, or to taste
1 tablespoon Italian parsley leaves and stems, finely chopped; plus 8 Italian parsley sprigs for garnish
2 tablespoons soy sauce
2 tablespoons dry sherry

Heat 2 tablespoons oil or butter in large saucepan over medium heat. Add mushrooms and stir quickly to distribute oil to all mushrooms. Cook, stirring frequently, for 2 minutes. Add onions, celery, and carrots. Cook, stirring occasionaly, for 5 minutes. Add scallions. Stir to mix; cook for 1 minute more, or until mushrooms are lightly brown and onions golden.

Remove vegetables from pan. Add remaining oil or butter. Stir in flour to make a roux; cook until flour bubbles and thickens. Whisk in broth a little at a time, taking care to avoid lumps. Return vegetables to broth. Add barley, bay leaves, thyme, lavender, pepper, chopped parsley, soy sauce, and sherry. Turn heat to low and simmer for about 2 hours, or until barley is tender. Serve in warmed soup bowls; garnish each with 2 mushroom slices and a parsley sprig.

Lavender-Scented Crabmeat Mousse

Make this yummy light mousse with luxurious lump crabmeat—lavender, dill, and chives add a touch of exotic flavor. Offer the mousse as an hors d'oeuvre with black bread or crackers; spoon it into ripe avocado halves as an appetizer or first course; or prepare it in individual decorative one-cup molds to present on a lettuce leaf or mixed greens as a light lunch. Serves 12 as an appetizer or first course, or 6–8 as a lunch.

1 envelope unflavored gelatin
¼ cup cold water
½ cup boiling water
½ cup light mayonnaise (or Miracle Whip)
1 tablespoon chopped fresh lavender flowers
2 tablespoons finely snipped fresh chives
2 tablespoons finely chopped fresh dill
1 tablespoon grated onion
1 tablespoon fresh lemon juice
Dash Tabasco sauce
⅓ teaspoon sweet or hot paprika
2 cups lump crabmeat, picked over for shells
1 cup heavy cream or whipping cream
Ruffled lettuce leaves
Fresh chives, dill sprigs, and lavender flowers for garnish

Soften gelatin in cold water in a large mixing bowl for 3 minutes. Stir in boiling water and whisk until gelatin dissolves. Cool to room temperature.

Add mayonnaise, chopped lavender flowers, snipped chives, chopped dill, grated onion, lemon juice, Tabasco, and paprika; whisk until completely blended. Refrigerate until slightly thickened, about 20 minutes.

Fold picked-over crabmeat into gelatin mixture. Whip cream in a separate bowl until it forms soft peaks. Fold gently into crab-gelatin mixture.

Pour mixture into a medium-sized bowl or a decorative 6–8 cup mold, using a rubber spatula to scrape all the mixture out of the large mixing bowl. Or if intended as a light lunch, pour into 6–8 individual decorative molds. Cover and refrigerate for at least 4 hours.

To serve, unmold mousse onto a lettuce-lined platter or individual plates and garnish with chives, dill sprigs, and lavender flowers.

Grilled Shrimp Aux Herbes

This is a great dish for a hot summer evening. Don't be put off by the full cup of oil–it's used only in the marinade. For a complete meal, grill skewers of peanut-oiled vegetables—mushrooms, bell peppers, onions, Japanese eggplant, zucchini and/or summer squash, and perhaps corn on the cob. Thread only one kind of vegetable per skewer for greater precision with cooking times for each veggie. After grilling, toss the cooked vegetables together in a large bowl so each person can select the ones he or she likes best or avoid those most unloved.

I use fresh herbs for this dish, usually a combination of Italian parsley, thyme, marjoram, and Greek or Mexican oregano; although I try to have about a tablespoon or two of each chopped herb to make about ½ cup total, the final proportions are whatever we have in the garden that's plentiful; use only ¼ cup total for dried herbs. The amount of lavender can vary—usually ½ teaspoon of chopped lavender leaves and 1 teaspoon chopped lavender flowers is enough for us. However, part of the fun of cooking is altering recipes to your own personal taste, so feel free to play with the amounts in this and any other recipe until it suits you. Serves 6.

> ½ cup extra-virgin olive oil (smell to be sure it's not rancid)
> ½ cup high-quality peanut oil (smell to be sure it's not rancid)
> ¼ cup minced fresh herbs (parsley, thyme, marjoram, oregano)
> ½ teaspoon minced fresh lavender leaves, or a pinch dried
> 1 teaspoon minced fresh lavender flowers, or ½ teaspoon dried
> ½ teaspoon red pepper flakes, or to taste
> 3 tablespoons lemon juice
> 3 garlic cloves, minced
> 1 tablespoon minced shallot or green onion
> freshly ground pepper
> 2 pounds large shrimp, shelled and deveined
> lemon wedges

Combine olive oil, peanut oil, minced herbs, minced lavender flowers, minced lavender leaves, red pepper flakes, lemon juice, minced garlic, minced shallot, and freshly ground pepper in a large bowl. Mix well.

Mix in shrimp, coating thoroughly. Cover with plastic wrap or bowl lid. Refrigerate several hours to marinate, stirring every hour or so.

Thread shrimp on 6 skewers. Prepare charcoal or gas grill; heat to cooking temperature. Add lavender grilling sticks (see p. 3) if desired. Grill shrimp skewers about 2 minutes on each side—do not overcook! Serve each person a shrimp skewer. Pass lemon wedges and veggie bowl as described in recipe introduction.

Suzanne's Orange Roughy in Lavender—Orange Wine Sauce

I invented this quick-to-fix dish on an evening when we had orange roughy but no thought as to a recipe except that it had to be fairly fast because it was already well past dinner time. Serve the fish with a wild rice combination and for an additional vegetable, saute fresh asparagus in a little butter or oil with sesame seeds and freshly ground pepper until just tooth tender. Serving more than two? The recipe doubles and triples easily. Serves 2

```
1 large or 2 small orange roughy fillets
fresh pepper to taste
1 cup fresh orange juice (2 oranges)
2 teaspoons dried culinary lavender
1 cup dry white wine
2 tablespoons orange liqueur
2 carrots, peeled and julienned
3 scallions, julienned
1 teaspoons unsalted butter or peanut oil
```

Pepper both sides of fish.

Squeeze orange juice and stir in lavender. Set aside to infuse lavender flavor into orange juice.

Peel carrots and trim ends off scallions. Cut carrots and scallions into 2-inch lengths. Julienne the pieces. Heat butter or peanut oil over medium heat; add julienned carrots and scallions and stir to coat. Cook about 5 minutes, stirring occasionally, or until veggies are tooth-tender.

Meanwhile, add white wine to orange juice and lavender. Bring to a boil in a pan suitable for poaching fish. Add fish and turn heat down to simmer. Poach fish until it barely flakes when tested with a fork, or until it is almost done to your liking. Remove fish to a warm plate or platter; cover and keep warm but not so hot as to continue cooking the fish.

Add orange liqueur to poaching liquid; turn up heat and reduce liquid by half. Return fish to pan until fish is just heated through.

Serve immediately: place fish on plates or platter. Top with veggies, and spoon sauce over all.

Broiled Salmon
with Lavender Champagne Sauce

This tasty salmon is an elegant dish for company, but it's also a great quick meal for the family. For an attractive presentation, serve it with colorful grilled mixed vegetables—perhaps a combination of baby carrots, baby squash, sliced red bell peppers, and sugar snap peas topped with a sprinkling of fresh corn kernels. You can broil the salmon under your oven's broiler or outside on a charcoal or gas grill. If you prefer a lighter sauce, use less butter. Serves 6.

6 6-ounce salmon fillets
olive oil
12 lavender sprigs for garnish

1 stick unsalted butter, cut into small pieces
½ cup minced shallots, white part only
⅓ cup dry Champagne or dry white wine
⅓ cup Champagne vinegar
⅓ cup fish stock, or 3 tablespoons clam juice and 2 tablespoons water
6 fresh lavender flower heads, chopped
freshly ground pepper

Prepare broiler (preheat indoor broiler or start fire in outdoor grill). Rub salmon fillets with olive oil and set aside.

In a saucepan, melt 1 tablespoon butter and add shallots. Cook, stirring frequently, until shallots are soft. Add champagne or wine, vinegar, and half the lavender. Raise heat to high, and cook until liquid is reduced to 3 or 4 tablespoons.

Turn off heat. Remove pan from heat, replacing pan with small saucepan to warm over residual heat. Whisk remaining butter into sauce a little at a time until well blended. Strain sauce through a fine sieve into the small saucepan. Add remaining lavender into sauce and season to taste with pepper. Keep warm.

Broil or grill salmon, basting occasionally with olive oil, for about 3–5 minutes per side, or until fish is flaky but not dry. Serve immediately, garnished with 2 crossed lavender sprigs, with the sauce on the side.

Lavender–Baked Scrod in Foil

This is a quick and easy dish that's as suitable for company as for a weeknight family dinner. What's more, baking in foil makes cleanup a breeze! Serve with buttered tender-crisp green beans, broccoli, or asparagus; baked potatoes with sour cream and fresh chives or new red potatoes steamed in their skins and tossed with chopped parsley; and a fresh, crunchy salad—sheer bliss! Serves 4, but can be modified easily for more or fewer.

4 scrod fillets, 4 to 6 ounces each
small amount of butter
2 medium carrots, julienned
1 large stalk celery, thinly sliced
1 medium onion, thinly sliced
1 tablespoon tiny capers, rinsed and drained
1 teaspoon dried thyme (leaf form, not ground)
½ teaspoon dried culinary lavender
4 thin slices lime
4 thin slices lemon
¼ cup dry sherry
freshly ground pepper
16 fresh chives
4 sprigs parsley

Preheat oven to 400°. Rinse scrod and pat dry with paper towels.

Cut four 18" x 12" pieces of heavy-duty foil. Lightly butter one side of each foil piece. Place a piece of fish in the center of each piece of foil. Sprinkle fish with carrots, celery, onions, capers, thyme, lavender, and freshly ground pepper. Top each with a lime slice and a lemon slice. Sprinkle with sherry.

Fold the edges of each foil packet tightly, leaving some air space in each packet to accommodate steam. Bake at 400° for 20-25 minutes, depending on desired degree of doneness.

Remove from oven. Let stand for 2-3 minutes. Carefully unwrap each packet and slide contents onto warmed dinner plates. Garnish top of each serving with four chives, crossed in an X pattern, and tuck a sprig of parsley along the side.

Lavender—Seared Ahi Tuna with Mustard Sauce

For this tasty dish, sear the tuna on the outside and leave the center cold and red. It's terrific served in winter atop a molded round of wild and brown rice mixed with vegetables or in summer over baby greens and edible flowers. The mustard sauce lends an added piquancy. I use a pepper mill set on the coarsest setting or a clean coffee grinder (don't overgrind!) to crush the peppercorns and fennel seeds. Serves 6.

For the mustard sauce:
2 tablespoons whole grain mustard
1 tablespoon olive oil
1 teaspoon mustard seeds, toasted
1 teaspoon rice wine vinegar
1 teaspoon lavender honey

For the tuna:
1¼ pounds ahi tuna, preferably as a sashimi block
1 tablespoon olive oil
2 teaspoons whole black peppercorns
1 teaspoon whole white peppercorns
2 teaspoons whole fennel seeds
1½ teaspoons dried lavender flowers
2 tablespoons peanut oil
Baby greens and edible flowers for summer
Molded rounds of wild and brown rice mixed with vegetables

Mix together all five ingredients for the mustard sauce; set aside.

In a pepper mill set to grind as coarsely as possible or in a clean coffee grinder, grind together black peppercorns, white peppercorns, fennel seeds, and dried lavender flowers. Lightly oil tuna block with 1 tablespoon olive oil, then coat with lavender-pepper-fennel mixture.

In a heavy skillet, heat peanut oil until just smoking. Quickly sear tuna block on all sides—no longer than 2 minutes total. For summer presentation, chill. For winter, keep warm.

To serve, thinly slice tuna into medallions, 3 or 4 per person. In summer, serve tuna cold on baby greens, drizzle with mustard sauce, and garnish with edible flowers. In winter, serve warm tuna on molded rice rounds, drizzle with mustard sauce, and garnish with vegetable slices.

Lavender Chicken with Rosemary and Lemon

This is what I call a "fix-it-and-forget-it" dish, easy and fast to prepare. You can make it a full meal by adding tiny carrots and new potatoes tossed in a little bit of melted butter to the pan about halfway through roasting the chicken. Microwave-steam some broccoli crowns for about 5 minutes for a pretty contrast to the rest of the meal. Use organic chicken if possible; it's healthier and tastes better Serves 2–4.

1 4– to 5–pound organic chicken
6 whole sprigs lavender
6 sprigs of rosemary, 3 inches long
½ lemon, thinly sliced
½ cup (or less) melted butter
sprig each rosemary and lavender for basting
tiny new red potatoes
baby carrots
sherry or white wine to deglaze pan
2 lavender sprigs for garnish

Preheat oven to 450º.

Rinse chicken with cold water and pat dry with paper towels. Place lavender, rosemary, and lemon slices in chicken cavity. Set chicken on rack in roasting pan, breast side up. Brush well with melted butter, using sprigs of lavender and rosemary as a brush.

Place in oven and immediately lower heat to 350º. Roast for about 20 minutes per pound, basting frequently with pan drippings, using the lavender and rosemary sprigs tied together as basting brush.

When there's about 40 minutes left to cook, you can add new potatoes and carrots around chicken.

The chicken is done when it is well browned and its joints move easily. It can cook a little longer if the potatoes aren't done. Remove chicken and vegetables from pan and deglaze pan with a little sherry or white wine.

Serve on a platter surrounded by carrots and potatoes drizzled with pan juices and sprinkled with chopped parsley. Cross two lavender sprigs over the top of the chicken for garnish.

Grilled Lamb Chops
with Herbes de Provence

These lamb chops are redolent of the scents and flavors of the hot, dry climate of the south of France—the Provence area famous for its herbs and local cooking. Good anytime, it's a great recipe for when spring lamb is plentiful and the weather is becoming pleasant for grilling outdoors. Serves 6.

> 12 organic lamb loin chops
> 3 cloves garlic, cut in half
> 3 teaspoons dried herbes de Provence (see p. 40)
> ¾ cup dry red wine
> 1 tablespoon butter
> pepper to taste
> 1 sprig each fresh rosemary and lavender for a basting brush
> sprigs of parsley, thyme, rosemary, or lavender for garnish
> lavender grilling sticks (p. 3)

Prepare outdoor grill so that coals are about medium to medium-high heat and grate is about 4 inches from coals. Rub chops on all sides with cut garlic.

In a small pan, combine *herbes de Provence*, wine, and butter. Heat until the butter melts. Brush some of the butter mixture on each chop, using a sprig of rosemary and a sprig of lavender as a basting brush.

Put chops on grill and watch meat closely, turning once, and basting often with butter mixture and combined-sprig brush. Grill 4 to 8 minutes per side, depending on heat of coals, thickness of meat, and how well-done you like your lamb. As you begin to cook the second side, toss a handful of lavender grilling sticks onto the coals for added flavor.

Sprinkle chops with pepper and serve immediately, garnished with herb sprigs.

Greek Lamb Chops with Lavender

My family is fond of lamb chops, and we're lucky enough to know Antonio Manzanares of Shepherd's Lamb in Tierra Amarilla, NM, who raises his sheep organically. This Greek-style recipe, a favorite at our house, sets off Antonio's superb loin lamb chops to perfection. Serves 4.

8 organic lamb loin chops, about 1"–1 ½" thick
12-16 cloves garlic, minced
1½ cups dry white wine
½ cup extra-virgin olive oil
8 tablespoons fresh lemon juice
1½ teaspoons dried oregano
1 teaspoon dried lavender
8–12 fresh sage leaves, finely chopped
1 tablespoon fresh rosemary leaves, chopped
freshly ground pepper
1 sprig each fresh rosemary and lavender for a basting brush
rosemary and lavender sprigs for garnish

Combine garlic, wine, olive oil, lemon juice, oregano, lavender, sage, rosemary, and pepper in a zippered plastic bag or large flat pan. Add lamb chops and let them marinate for at least 30 minutes.

Prepare charcoal grill for cooking and light coals. When grill is ready (about 30 minutes), drain lamb chops and place them on grill over hot coals. As meat surfaces dry, baste with marinade, using a basting brush make of rosemary and lavender sprigs. Cook to desired degree of doneness, turning once; if desired, toss lavender grilling sticks (p. 3) on coals as you turn the meat. Serve two chops per person, garnishing each serving with crossed sprigs of rosemary and lavender.

Grilled Marinated Filets Mignons on Lavender Foil Bread

A super dish for summer entertaining or just for a quick meal. Serve with steamed broccoli florets tossed with grated lemon zest and a dab of melted butter. The recipe can be doubled or halved. Serves 6.

For filets mignons:

> 6 bacon-wrapped filets mignons
> 1 cup dry red wine
> 1 tablespoon low-sodium soy sauce
> 2 tablespoons dry sherry
> 1 teaspoon dried thyme leaves, crumbled
> 1 teaspoon dried whole lavender (flowers and leaves)
> ¼ teaspoon freshly ground pepper (coarsely ground)
> 18 large whole mushrooms cooked in butter and sherry for garnish

Place filets mignons in a zippered plastic bag. Add wine, soy sauce, sherry, thyme leaves, lavender, and pepper. Marinate, turning frequently, for 30–60 minutes.

Meanwhile, prepare charcoal grill and lavender foil bread (see recipe below). When meat has marinated, cook over coals, turning once, until meat has reached the desired degree of doneness.

Serve each atop a slice of foil bread and garnish with mushrooms.

For Lavender Foil Bread:

> 1 loaf sourdough French bread
> 1 stick butter or margarine, softened to room temperature
> 1 scant tablespoon dried lavender
> 1 heaping tablespoon finely chopped parsley
> 1 heaping tablespoon finely chopped chives
> 1 heaping tablespoon finely chopped celery leaves
> 1 red onion, thinly sliced
> processed Monterey Jack cheese, thinly sliced

Preheat oven to 400º. Combine butter, lavender, parsley, chives, and celery leaves. Slice bread in ¾–inch slices, place on a cookie sheet, and spread with butter mixture. Place thin slices of onion and cheese on each slice. Cover cookie sheet with foil and heat in a 400% oven until cheese melts and bread is hot, about 20 minutes. Place 1 slice under each filet mignon. Wrap leftovers tightly in foil. Later, top with tomato and more cheese; run under broiler to make open-faced sandwiches.

Lavender—Laced Filets Mignons with Mushroom Sauce

This any-season recipe can be doubled, tripled, or more. Serve the filets mignons with buttered steamed new potatoes and parsley or steak fries done in the oven; steamed fresh green beans and grated orange zest drizzled with freshly squeezed orange juice; and a simple dessert of ice cream. You can order lavender grilling sticks and Herbes de Santa Fe from For the Love of Lavender (see p. 3). Serves 2.

2 bacon-wrapped filets mignons
lavender grilling sticks (p. 3)—a bunch about the size of a nickel
red table wine to cover lavender sticks
10 cloves garlic
2 cups red table wine for steak marinade
2 tablespoons *Herbes de Santa Fe* with green chile
1 teaspoon lavender
¼ teaspoon coarse-grind black pepper
¼ teaspoon red pepper flakes
1 tablespoon butter
1 cup sliced mushrooms (domestic or wild)

Break the lavender sticks in half and place in a long, narrow container (I use a corn-on-the-cob dish) and cover with red table wine. Set aside.

Mince garlic cloves. To zippered plastic bag, add red table wine, minced garlic, *Herbes de Santa Fe*, lavender, black pepper, and red pepper flakes. Close bag; shake it to mix contents well. Add filets mignons. Close bag and squeeze out excess air as you close zipper. Knead bag to distribute marinade and seasonings evenly over filets. Set aside to marinate for 30–45 minutes, turning bag every ten minutes or so.

Prepare charcoal grill and light fire. Leave cooking grate off for now.

Meanwhile, melt butter in small skillet over medium-low heat. Add mushrooms; quickly stir to coat all pieces with melted butter. Turn up heat to medium. Sauté mushrooms until lightly browned; remove mushrooms to a small bowl.

For sauce, boil off any liquid in the pan. Deglaze pan with liquid from lavender sticks, scraping up all the brown bits. Strain meat marinade into frying pan. Turn heat to high and reduce liquid by half. Return mushrooms to sauce liquid, turn heat down to low, and continue to simmer sauce.

Place moist lavender sticks on hot coals. Place grate over coals. Place filets mignons on cooking grate; grill to desired doneness, about 3 minutes per side for medium rare, depending on how hot the fire is.

Serve filets on individual plates with mushroom sauce poured over.

Sautéed Veal Scallops
with Lavender—Lemon Sauce

This recipe is both simple to prepare and elegant in presentation, making it a perfect dish for a special cozy Saturday night dinner with good friends. Serves 6.

12 3-ounce veal scallops
4 tablespoons flour, seasoned with freshly ground pepper
2 tablespoons clarified butter
2 tablespoons chopped shallots
¾ cup dry white wine
¼ cup lemon juice
2 tablespoons fresh lavender flowers, chopped
½ cup brown veal stock
2 tablespoons unsalted butter
lemon wedges and lavender sprigs for garnish

Pound veal scallops to a uniform thickness and dredge them in seasoned flour.

Heat clarified butter in a sauté pan. Add scallops to pan in a single layer. Sauté for 1–2 minutes on each side. Remove to warm platter and sauté remaining scallops. Remove to warm platter.

Add chopped shallots to pan and sauté until shallots begin to turn translucent.

Add white wine and lemon juice to deglaze pan. Add lavender flowers, stirring constantly until lavender flowers are coated with liquid.

Add brown veal stock and reduce resulting liquid by half, stirring frequently.

Blend in butter, stirring constantly. Adjust seasoning if necessary.

To serve, place two scallops on plate and drizzle on about a tablespoon of sauce. Garnish with lemon wedges and lavender sprigs.

Pasta with Fresh Herbs

You can make this wonderfully quick dish as a simple light meal for lunch or dinner. You can make it heartier with the addition of sautéed skinless chicken breast pieces, shrimp, crabmeat, or lobster chunks. An idea for a quick vegetarian meal is to mix in some combination of fresh or frozen organic vegetables. Add a green salad and some crusty bread fresh from the oven or breadmaker to round out the meal. Any pasta will do, but the sauce lends itself especially well to linguine, fettuccine, or bow ties. Serves 4–6.

Linguine, fettuccine, or bow ties made with 100% durum semolina flour
3 tablespoons butter
1 cup heavy cream
½ cup grated Parmesan cheese
1 tablespoon chopped lavender flowers
1 tablespoon chopped fresh sweet marjoram
1 tablespoon chopped fresh parsley
1 tablespoon chopped fresh sweet basil
1 tablespoon snipped fresh chives
several grindings of black or combo-colored peppercorns, to taste
(optional) cooked chicken breast pieces, shrimp, crabmeat, or lobster chunks
(optional) colorful frozen mixed vegetables
grated Parmesan cheese for topping
chopped herbs for topping
4–6 fresh lavender sprigs with flowers, for garnish

Cook pasta in a large pot of boiling salted water until just tooth tender; drain.

Melt butter in a large sauté pan. Add cream, ½ cup grated Parmesan cheese, lavender flowers, sweet marjoram, parsley, sweet basil, chives, and freshly ground pepper. Stir to blend thoroughly. Simmer sauce until somewhat thickened, enough to coat a spoon.

Add pasta to sauce and toss until pasta is well-coated. Add optional chicken, seafood, or vegetables. Serve immediately in pasta dishes. Top with more Parmesan cheese and sprinkle with chopped herbs. Garnish each serving with a sprig of lavender leaves and flowers.

New Potatoes with Lemon—Lavender—Chive Butter

This side dish is especially nice with spring lamb, fish, seafood, and chicken. Serves 6.

    24 small red new potatoes
    3 tablespoons unsalted butter
    2 tablespoons chopped fresh lavender flowers
    2 tablespoons chopped fresh chives
    1 tablespoon fresh lemon juice
    freshly ground pepper

Peel a thin strip around the middle of each potato, leaving the rest of the skin intact. In a large saucepan over high heat, place potatoes in enough water to cover. Bring to a boil. Reduce heat and cook, covered, about 15 minutes, or until potatoes are just tender. Drain potatoes.

Turn heat to low. Over low heat, melt butter in pan. Add lavender, chives, lemon juice, and pepper to taste. Stir to mix. Return potatoes to pan and toss gently in butter mixture until potatoes are well coated.

Lavender—Fried Apples

This recipe came about because I was serving a pork roast and decided it called for something a little sweet and tart. Applesauce came to mind, but I wanted something different, a little out of the ordinary. Hence this recipe was born. Serves 6 as an accompaniment to roast pork.

> ½ teaspoon dried lavender flowers
> 2 tablespoons sugar
> ¾ teaspoon ground nutmeg
> ¾ teaspoon ground cinnamon
> ½ teaspoon finely shredded orange or lemon rind, colored part only
> 6 medium to large cooking apples, washed, cored, and sliced into ½–inch rings
> 6 tablespoons unsalted butter

Combine lavender flowers with sugar, nutmeg, and cinnamon. To make shredded orange or lemon rind, scrape the whole orange or lemon over the fine shredding blade on a grater just until the white begins to show through. Add shredded orange rind and toss together.

Melt butter in a large skillet over moderate heat. Add apple rings. Sprinkle half the lavender-sugar mixture over apple slices. Fry for 3 to 4 minutes. Turn slices gently with a spatula. Sprinkle remaining lavender-sugar mixture over slices. Continue to cook until apples are soft but not so long that the rings fall apart.

Mediterranean Carrots

Make this flavorful vegetable dish as a simple accompaniment to poultry, ham, beef, or vegetarian dinners. Be sure you know the intensity of your dried lavender so it doesn't overpower the carrots. The citrus juices add tartness, and the toasted pine nuts add a bit of crunch. Serves 6 as a side dish.

12 carrots, peeled and cut into thick slices (about ½ inch)
5 tablespoons unsalted butter
½ to 1 teaspoon dried lavender
freshly ground pepper to taste
1 tablespoon unsalted butter
¼ cup fresh lemon juice
1 tablespoon fresh orange juice
2 tablespoons brown sugar
1 cup pine nuts, toasted
3 tablespoons chopped parsley
parsley sprigs for garnish

In a large, heavy saucepan, bring 8 cups of water to boil. Add a pinch of salt. Blanch carrots for 3 minutes. Drain.

Melt 5 tablespoons butter over medium-low heat. Add carrots and cook, tossing with a rubber spatula every few minutes until carrots are tender to taste.

Reduce heat to very low. Add 1 tablespoon butter. Sprinkle carrots with dried lavender. Toss to coat carrots with butter-lavender mixture. Add lemon juice, orange juice, and brown sugar. Heat, tossing occasionally, until carrots are glazed. Sprinkle with toasted pine nuts and parsley and toss to combine. Garnish with parsley sprigs. Serve at once.

Lavender Peas

This is a long-time favorite vegetable recipe. It's wonderful with lamb or chicken, and it's especially good with Grilled Lamb Chops (p. 18) or Greek Lamb Chops (p. 19). Serves 6.

2 10-ounce packages frozen peas, or equivalent amount of freshly shelled garden peas
¼ teaspoon sugar, scant
¼ teaspoon salt, scant
¼ teaspoon freshly ground pepper
1 tablespoon unsalted butter or extra virgin olive oil
¾ teaspoon lemon juice
1 tablespoon fresh lavender stalks, minced; or 1 teaspoon whole dried lavender, crushed
lavender sprigs and lemon peel strips, yellow part only, for garnish

Cook peas in a little water with sugar and salt to keep their bright green color. Drain well. Toss peas with pepper, butter, lemon juice, and lavender. Heat until thoroughly blended. Transfer to warmed serving bowl and garnish with lavender sprigs and lemon peel strips.

Zucchini Provençal

This is a great way to use ever-abundant zucchini. The secret to success with this dish is to take great care not to overcook the zucchini—it should be tender-crisp and toothsome. Be sparing with the lavender leaves because of their strong flavor. Serves 4–6.

1 tablespoon extra-virgin olive oil
3 green onions, thinly sliced
2 cloves garlic, finely minced
5 small zucchini, sliced
2 ripe tomatoes, peeled, seeded, and chopped
1 tablespoon chopped fresh parsley
1 tablespoon chopped fresh oregano
1 tablespoon chopped fresh basil
1½ teaspoons chopped fresh lavender flowers
¼ teaspoon chopped fresh lavender leaves
1–2 cups shredded low-fat mozzarella cheese
fresh basil sprigs for garnish

Preheat the broiler.

On stovetop in an oven-proof pan, sauté onion until it turns translucent; add garlic and sauté for thirty seconds. Add sliced zucchini and stir-fry with a rubber cooking spatula (be sure it will take high temperatures) only until tender-crisp.

Add chopped tomatoes, parsley, oregano, basil, and lavender flowers and leaves; cook, stirring, for about a minute or a little more, until tomatoes are hot. Turn off heat.

Immediately sprinkle with mozzarella cheese. Transfer pan to oven; broil until cheese is melted and browning slightly. Tuck a basil sprig or two at edge of pan for ganish. Serve at once from the pan.

Lavender Crêpes Suzanne

This is my variation of the classic French dessert, Crêpes Suzette. Makes 15 crêpes, serving 4–6.

For the crêpes:

 1 tablespoon brandy
 2 teaspoons fresh lavender flowers, chopped, or 1 teaspoon dried
 6 eggs
 4 tablespoons flour, sifted twice
 2 tablespoons cold water
 ¼ teaspoon salt
 1 tablespoon sugar
 1 tablespoon butter

Place brandy in a small cup. Add lavender flowers and set aside for at least 20 minutes to infuse brandy with lavender flavor.

Meanwhile, place 6 eggs in mixing bowl with flour, cold water, salt, and sugar. Beat well until batter consistency reaches that of heavy cream. Chill in refrigerator 15 minutes.

Remove batter from refrigerator. Squeeze brandy–lavender mixture through cheesecloth into batter. Mix well.

In a small frying pan or crêpe pan, melt butter. When butter begins to bubble, pour in about 1 tablespoon of batter and swirl quickly in the pan to make the crêpe as thin as possible. Brown lightly, flip over and brown other side, then slide onto a warmed platter. Repeat with remaining batter.

For sauce:

 ½ cup unsalted butter
 ½ cup confectioners' sugar
 1 teaspoon fresh chopped lavender flowers
 grated peel of 1 orange
 juice of same orange
 1 teaspoon lemon juice
 ¼ cup orange liqueur
 ¼ cup brandy

Butter a chafing dish; set it over water simmering water.

Cream together butter and sugar. Blend in lavender flowers and grated orange peel. Work in orange juice, lemon juice, and orange liqueur. Spread mixture on crêpes and fold them in quarters. Arrange in buttered chafing dish. Sprinkle with sugar and brandy. Ignite brandy and serve flaming.

Lavender Pound Cake

Lavender gives this pound cake a touch of the Mediterranean. Serve it plain, with ice cream, or perhaps topped with fresh sliced strawberries. Makes one 10-inch cake.

2 cups butter, softened
3¾ cups all-purpose flour
1 teaspoon baking powder
12 large eggs, separated
2½ cups sugar
2 tablespoons sweet sherry
1 tablespoon dried lavender flowers

Preheat oven to 350°. Liberally grease and lightly flour a 10-inch tube or bundt pan.

In a large bowl, cream butter until it is light and fluffy. Combine flour and baking powder and gradually add to butter, beating until mixture is a smooth paste.

In another large bowl, combine egg yolks and sugar. Beat until thick and light. Add sherry and lavender. Gradually beat in butter and flour mixture.

In a separate bowl with clean, dry beaters, beat egg whites until they form stiff peaks but are not dry. Gently fold beaten egg whites into flour mixture. Scoop batter into the tube or bundt cake pan. Bake 1 hour 15 minutes, or until a straw inserted in the center comes out clean.

Lavender–Apple Pound Cake

Bake this easy, moist, lavender-scented pound cake in your prettiest six-inch round cake mold for your next dinner party, potluck, hostess gift, or bake sale. Bound to be a winner! Serves 6.

3 large eggs
1 cup sugar
1¼ cup all-purpose flour
⅛ teaspoon baking powder
⅔ cup corn or peanut oil (or melted butter or margarine)
½ large apple, peeled, cored, quartered, and cut into slices
½ teaspoon grated lemon zest
1–2 tablespoons dried lavender flowers
2 tablespoons kirsch or other liqueur, plus some for garnish

Preheat oven to 375°. Butter and sugar a 6-inch round, 3-inch high cake mold.

In a large bowl, combine eggs, sugar, flour, baking powder, and oil. Add apple, lemon zest, lavender, and kirsch. Mix well. Pour into prepared mold. Bake until golden and firm, about 35 minutes. Unmold and cool on a rack.

Cut into six wedges and serve, drizzled with liqueur.

Lavender Mini–Meringues

These yummy little confections are a real delight. You can store them in your freezer for up to three months, so you'll always be ready with a dessert to serve unexpected guests. Makes 3 dozen; serves 12 with three mini-meringues per serving.

1 cup granulated sugar
¼ cup dried lavender flowers
1½ cups confectioners' sugar
6 egg whites, room temperature
Chambord or Framboise, or other fruit liqueur
To serve 6 persons, 18 raspberries, small strawberries, or other berries
6 sprigs of lavender or mint for garnish

Preheat oven to 225°. Line a cookie sheet with baking parchment.

Whirl lavender and granulated sugar in a blender or food processor until the lavender is pulverized. Sift into a bowl with the confectioners' sugar.

With an electric or hand mixer, beat egg whites until soft peaks form. Gradually add sugar mixture, beating constantly; beat until stiff peaks form.

Drop by teaspoonfuls onto parchment-lined cookie sheet. Press lightly with thumb to make a small cup-like indentation. Bake 2 hours at 225°, or until crisp but still pastel blue, not browned.

To serve, drizzle a small amount of Chambord or Framboise around the edge of a dessert plate. Place three mini-meringues in the center of the plate. Place a raspberry, strawberry, or other berry in the indentation of each mini-meringue. Garnish each plate with a sprig of lavender or mint.

Lavender Shortbread Cookies

This shortbread cookie is a superb addition to the tea table, and it's lovely with a bowl of fresh strawberries for breakfast. Good plain or iced with lavender-flavored icing (below). Makes 18–24 cookies.

½ cup unsalted butter, softened
½ cup solid vegetable shortening or unsalted margarine, softened
½ – ⅔ cup granulated sugar
1 teaspoon vanilla extract
2 tablespoons fresh lemon juice or ¼ teaspoon lemon extract
2 cups all-purpose flour
1 tablespoon dried lavender flowers
⅛ teaspoon salt

Preheat oven to 325°.

In a medium mixing bowl, cream together butter, shortening or margarine, sugar, and vanilla. Add lemon juice and mix thoroughly. Add flour and mix until dough is smooth. Dough should be soft but not sticky; if it feels sticky, add up to an additional ¼ cup flour. Chill 2 hours to firm.

On a lightly floured surface, roll dough out to ¼ inch thick. Cut into shapes with cookie cutters. Place on ungreased cookie sheet. Re-roll remaining dough and cut out shapes. Bake at 325° for 10–15 minutes, or until cookies are lightly browned around the edges. Cool completely on rack. Ice or decorate if you wish.

Lavender Cookie Icing:

1 cup lavender confectioners' sugar (make at least 1 day ahead)
2 teaspoons milk
2 teaspoons light corn syrup
violet icing color (optional)
crystallized lavender blossoms (optional)

To make lavender confectioner's sugar: mix 2 tablespoons lavender with 1 cup confectioners sugar in small bowl. Let stand, covered, at least 24 hours.

While cookies are cooling, combine lavender sugar, milk, and corn syrup. Mix well. Stir in violet icing color if desired. Spread on cookies. Top each cookie with two or three crystallized lavender blossoms if desired.

Lavender Cookies

An all-around cookie, not too sweet, just right to serve with tea or lemonade. Makes about 4 dozen cookies.

> ½ cup unsalted butter, softened
> 1 cup sugar
> 2 eggs
> ½ teaspoon vanilla extract
> 1 teaspoon dried lavender flowers, finely chopped
> 1¾ cups all-purpose flour
> 1 teaspoon baking powder

Preheat oven to 375º.

In a medium bowl, cream butter and sugar until light and fluffy. Beat in eggs, vanilla, and lavender; mix well.

Combine flour and baking powder. Add to lavender mixture, stirring until well blended.

Drop by teaspoonsful onto an ungreased baking sheet. Bake 8–10 minutes, or until lightly browned around the edges. Cool on baking sheet for 1–2 minutes, then transfer to a rack to finish cooling.

Cherries with Lavender Flowers

This is a wonderful mid-summer dessert. You can serve it two ways, and both are crowd pleasers. Either serve the cherries in pretty dessert bowls, or serve them over a rich French-vanilla ice cream. Serves 6–8.

1½ cups water
½ cup sugar
2 tablespoons fresh lavender flowers
2¼ pounds fresh cherries, stemmed
fresh lavender flower sprigs or mint sprigs for garnish

In a saucepan over high heat, combine water, sugar, and lavender flowers. Bring to a boil, and continue to boil for 10 minutes, stirring occasionally. Remove from heat and let stand for 10 minutes. Strain, discarding lavender.

Return syrup to saucepan, add cherries, and bring to a boil. Immediately remove from heat, cover, and cool to room temperature. Chill in refrigerator until ready to serve.

Serve either alone or over ice cream. Garnish with lavender flower sprigs or mint sprigs.

Lavender Lemonade

Lovely to look at, delightful to smell, and heaven to taste—what more could anyone ask of a cooling drink on a warm summer evening? The flower petals lend a pink color to the lemonade, but the beverage is just as good without them. Serves 6.

> 5 cups water
> 1½ cups sugar
> petals of red roses, rose geraniums, or hibiscus (optional)
> 12 blooming stems fresh lavender
> 2¼ cups fresh lemon juice
> 6 blooming lavender sprigs for garnish

In a medium saucepan, combine 2½ cups water with sugar and flower petals. Bring to a boil while stirring to dissolve sugar. Simmer for a few minutes longer to extract color from flower petals. Remove from heat and stir in lavender. Cover and let cool.

When syrup is cool, strain into a large pitcher. Add remaining 2½ cups water and lemon juice. Taste for sweetness and add more sugar if desired. Refrigerate until serving time.

Just before serving, add ice cubes. Pour into chilled glasses and garnish each with a lavender sprig.

Lavender Lapsang—Souchong Tea

This is one of my wild ideas, invented on a cold winter day when I wanted a really hearty cup of tea. Perhaps not to everyone's taste, Lapsang-Souchong is a very smokey, robust black tea from China, where they say only men drink it—and then only the men with strong stomachs. I thought the addition of lavender flowers would add a feminine touch. Make a single cup or a whole pot, as you choose.

> a kettle of water heated to just below boiling
> Lapsang—Souchong tea leaves, to your taste
> ⅛ to ¼ teaspoon dried lavender flowers, or more to your taste
> few drops fresh lemon juice

In a kettle, heat water to just below boiling. Place tea leaves and lavender flowers in a tea infuser or tea ball.

Fill china, porcelain, or pottery cup or teapot with hot water. Swirl hot water around the cup or teapot and let it heat for a minute or so. Pour out water.

Place filled tea infuser or tea ball in the heated cup or teapot. Pour hot water over tea infuser. Steep tea to desired strength. Add a few drops of fresh lemon juice. If using a teapot, serve tea in warmed cups.

Lavender—Spice Mixtures

Make these three spice mixtures with a kiss of Provence to liven up otherwise bland recipes. For storage, use clean empty glass herb jars with lids. Crush them coarsely in a clean coffee grinder or pepper mill before adding to your recipes.

Lavender-Spice Mixture No. 1:
Add some zing to fish and seafood recipes—use this blend as a rub for pan-fried fish or add it to recipes toward the end of cooking.

> ½ teaspoon fennel seeds
> 1 teaspoon dried thyme
> ¼ teaspoon ground cumin
> ⅛ teaspoon crushed allspice berries
> ¼ teaspoon chopped dried lemon peel
> ¼ teaspoon dried rosemary
> ¼ teaspoon dried lavender flowers
> ¼ teaspoon freshly ground pepper
> Pinch saffron threads
> Pinch crushed bay leaves

Mix well and store covered at room temperature for up to a month. When ready to use, crush desired amount in a clean coffee grinder or pepper mill before adding to recipe. Makes 1 tablespoon.

Lavender-Spice Mixture No. 2:
Great for grilling or barbecuing meat and fish. Sprinkle on meat or fish toward the end of cooking, or for a heavenly aroma, try sprinkling a little over the coals as you put the meat or fish on the grill.

> ½ teaspoon ground cumin
> 1 tablespoon dried thyme
> ½ teaspoon dried rosemary
> 1 teaspoon dried lavender flowers
> ¼ teaspoon chopped dried orange zest
> ½ teaspoon dried sage
> ½ teaspoon freshly ground pepper

Mix well and store covered at room temperature for up to a month. When ready to use, crush desired amount in a clean coffee grinder or pepper mill before adding to recipe. Makes 3 tablespoons.

Lavender-Spice Mixture No. 3:
Add this mixture to recipes toward the end of cooking to make ordinary vegetables come alive.

½ teaspoon dried thyme
¼ teaspoon dried rosemary
½ teaspoon dried parsley (or fresh, if using immediately)
½ teaspoon dried minced scallion (or fresh, if using immediately)
⅛ teaspoon curry powder
⅛ teaspoon minced dried lemon peel
¼ teaspoon freshly ground pepper
¼ teaspoon dried lavender flowers
Pinch saffron threads
Pinch crushed bay leaves
Pinch garlic powder

Mix well and store covered at room temperature for up to a month. When ready to use, crush desired amount in a mortar with pestle or grind in a clean coffee mill before adding to recipe. Makes 1 tablespoon (scant).

Herbes de Provence

This seasoning is both expensive to buy in specialty stores and wildly varying in quality and content. However, it's easy to make at home with dried herbs readily available in your cupboard or at your grocer's. The signature ingredient in herbes de Provence is lavender flowers.

Herbes de Provence, Recipe I:
Makes ⅓ cup.

> 3 tablespoons dried marjoram
> 3 tablespoons thyme
> 2 tablespoons dried summer savory
> 1½ teaspoons dried rosemary
> ½ teaspoon dried sage
> ½ teaspoon dried mint
> ½ teaspoon fennel seeds
> ¼ teaspoon dried lavender flowers

Combine marjoram, thyme, summer savory, rosemary, sage, mint, fennel seeds, and lavender flowers; mix well. Store in a covered glass jar. Crush desired amount in a clean coffee grinder or pepper mill before using.

Herbes de Provence, Recipe II:
Makes ½ cup.

> 4 tablespoons thyme
> 2 tablespoons rosemary
> 1 tablespoon lavender
> 1 tablespoon fennel seeds
> 3 bay leaves, crushed

Combine thyme, rosemary, lavender, fennel seeds, and bay leaves; mix well. Store in a covered glass jar. Crush desired amount in a clean coffee grinder or pepper mill before using.

Lavender Butters

Try these lavender-scented butters as a topping for breads, fish, or grilled meats.

Lavender Butter No. 1:

> 1 stick unsalted butter, at room temperature
> 2 tablespoons finely minced lavender flowers
> ¼ teaspoon grated fresh lemon zest
> ⅛ teaspoon fresh lemon juice

Cream butter until light and fluffy, then work in the lavender and lemon zest. Stir in the lemon juice. Use as a spread for breads or muffins.

Lavender Butter No. 2:

> 1 stick unsalted butter, at room temperature
> 1 tablespoon finely chopped lavender leaves
> 1 teaspoon finely chopped rosemary leaves
> 1 teaspoon finely chopped sage leaves
> freshly ground pepper
> 6 juniper berries, pounded (optional)
> 2 garlic cloves, pounded until smooth (optional)

Cream the butter until light and fluffy, then stir in the rest of the ingredients. This is good with lamb and game.

Lavender Butter No. 3:

> 1 stick unsalted butter, at room temperature
> 2 tablespoons finely chopped mixed fresh herbs
> > (parsley, chervil, tarragon, chives, and oregano)
> 1 tablespoon finely chopped lavender flowers and leaves
> 1 teaspoon lemon juice
> 1 large shallot, minced
> 1 garlic clove, minced to a puree
> freshly ground pepper

Work the herbs into the butter; gradually add lemon juice. Stir in shallot, garlic, and pepper. Good with meat and poultry.

Lavender Butter No. 4:

> 1 stick unsalted butter, at room temperature
> 2 tablespoons (total) finely chopped basil, chives, and thyme
> 2 tablespoons finely chopped lavender blossoms
> ½ teaspoon lemon juice

Cream the butter with the herbs and lavender blossoms. Stir in lemon juice and blend well. Add pinch white pepper if desired. Good with fish.

Lavender-Herb Cheese Spread

Make this great-tasting spread from those chunks of leftover cheese in your refrigerator. Use at least three different kinds; up to seven kinds and textures will work. If the cheese has been there for awhile, trim off any mold or dry parts, and taste a little to be sure it hasn't picked up any off flavorings from other denizens of the refrigerator. This spread is good at room temperature, but it's especially yummy spread on the cracker of your choice and run under the broiler briefly until it begins to melt.

1 pound, total, of 3 to 7 different kinds and textures of leftover cheese
6 garlic cloves, peeled
¾ cup dry white wine.
2 teaspoons chopped fresh lavender leaves, or 1 teaspoon dry lavender leaves
¼ teaspoon hot red pepper flakes
1 teaspoon freshly ground black or multicolored pepper

Coarsely chop garlic cloves in a food processor. Add cheese and coarsely chop. Add wine, lavender, red pepper flakes, and ground pepper. Process until soft and creamy, about 30–45 seconds. Refrigerate in a tightly covered bowl. Bring to room temperature before serving.

Variation: To make this recipe into a dip, add ½ cup sour cream or yogurt to the food processor mixture before refrigerating.

Lavender Kisses

These lavender kisses are a lovely accompaniment for a dessert like chocolate mousse, a parfait of orange sherbert with mandarin oranges and whipped cream, or a chilled banana pudding. Serve the dessert in stemmed glasses atop a lace-paper doily on a glass plate, with a lavender strip and a few of the lavender kisses stacked on the plate.

1 cup granulated sugar
  ¼ cup dried lavender flowers
  1½ cups powdered sugar
  6 egg whites, room temperature

Preheat oven to 225º.
  Pulverize lavender and granular sugar in food processor. Sift into bowl with powdered sugar.
  Beat egg whites with electric mixer until soft peaks form. Gradually add sugar mixture and beat until stiff peaks form.
  Drop by spoonfuls onto parchment-covered cookie sheet. Flatten slightly. Bake for 2 hours at 225º. Should be crisp but still pastel blue. Makes 36.

Lavender Watermelon Salad

Serve this scrumptious composed salad on your deck or patio to cool off after a hot summer day. It's equally refreshing indoors. The recipe is designed to serve as many as you choose, so the amounts given below are "per person."

For salad:
 1 cup 1-inch watermelon cubes, seeds and rind removed
 4 medium-to-large radishes, thinly sliced
 2 cups baby salad greens, loosely packed
 ¼ cup crumbled feta cheese
 5 fresh mint leaves, chopped
 5 fresh lavender leaves, chopped
 ½ teaspoon fresh lavender flowers, picked from the stem
 Fresh-ground black pepper to taste
 Mint leaf and lavender sprig for garnish

For dressing:
 ¼ teaspoon dried lavender flowers, pulverized with mortar and pestle
 1 tablespoon red balsamic vinegar
 1 tablespoon extra-virgin olive oil

Make dressing first. Pulverize dried lavender flowers. In a salad dressing bottle, combine balsamic vinegar, olive oil, and pulverized lavender flowers. Shake well to mix thoroughly.
  Place salad greens on chilled salad plate. Combine watermelon and radishes on top. Sprinkle with chopped mint and lavender leaves. Top with feta cheese and fresh lavender flowers. Drizzle with the dressing. Garnish with mint leaf and lavender sprig. Serves 1.

Lavender and Buttermilk Fried Chicken

This is a great dish served hot or cold with potato salad, chilled three-bean salad, and watermelon for a marvelous picnic on the deck or the beach.

3 whole chicken breasts, split in half
2 teaspoons freshly ground black pepper, divided
1 teaspoon dried lavender flowers, pulverized
2 cups buttermilk
Canola or peanut oil for frying
2 cups flour
1 teaspoon hot paprika
¼ teaspoon cayenne pepper
1 teaspoon dried thyme
2 tablespoons dried lavender flowers, crushed
2 large eggs
1 cup milk
1 cup water

Rub the chicken pieces with 1 teaspoon of the ground black pepper and crushed dried lavender flowers. Put buttermilk in zippered plastic bag. Add chicken and marinate 12 hours or overnight in refrigerator.

Heat oil in large frypan. Meanwhile in large bowl, combine flour, hot paprika, cayenne pepper, thyme, lavender flowers, and remaining 1 teaspoon pepper. In a separate bowl, whisk eggs, milk, and water until smooth.

Remove chicken from marinade. Shake off buttermilk. Dredge each chicken piece in flour mixture to coat, dip into egg batter, and dredge again with flour mixture.

Place chicken carefully in hot oil. Fry, uncovered, for 10–12 minutes. Carefully flip to other side and fry for 10–12 minutes more, or until golden brown and crispy. Remove from oil and drain on paper towels. Serve immediately. Serves 6.

Barb's Strawberry-Lavender Coffee Cake

Wonderful for brunch or mid-afternoon tea, this easy-to-make coffee cake sings of balmy days and flowers.

Batter:
- 2 ¼ cups flour
- ¾ cup sugar
- ¾ cup butter (1½ stick)
- ½ teaspoon baking powder
- ½ teaspoon baking soda
- ¾ cup buttermilk
- 1 egg, slightly beaten
- 2 tablespoons lavender buds, ground coarsely or crumbled

Filling:
- 2 cups sliced fresh strawberries plus a few strawberries to slice for garnish
- ¼ cup sugar
- 1 tablespoon corn starch
- 2 teaspoons lavender buds (whole)
- Fresh lavender sprigs for garnish

Preheat oven to 350°. Grease 8-inch-square baking dish.

Combine flour and sugar in large bowl. Cut in the butter until mixture is crumbly. Reserve ½ cup of mixture.

Add baking powder and baking soda to remaining mixture and stir in.

Combine buttermilk and egg. Add dry ingredient mixture and stir until just moistened.

In a bowl large enough to fit, combine sliced strawberries, sugar, and corn starch.

Put two-thirds of the batter into greased 8-inch-square baking dish. Spread with strawberry filling. Drop remaining batter by spoonfuls on top of filling. Sprinkle with reserved crumbly mixture.

Bake at 350° for 35–40 minutes, or until golden brown. Serve on pretty china or a glass plate topped with a lace-paper doily. Garnish with a few sliced strawberries and a lavender sprig. Makes 1 8-inch square coffee cake.

Skinny Strawberry-Lavender Tiramisu

This easy dessert is delicious and guilt-free. Serve atop lace-paper doilies on glass plates, garnished with a sprinkle of chocolate shavings and sprigs of fresh lavender and mint.

2½ cups stemmed, sliced strawberries, ½ cup reserved
2 8-ounce packages reduced-fat cream cheese
¾ cup powdered sugar
2 teaspoons dried lavender flowers, pulverized in a mortar
1 8-ounce container frozen whipped topping, thawed
1 cup strong coffee, room temperature
3 tablespoons coffee-flavored liqueur
24 lady fingers, split in half, or pound cake cut into ¾ -inch slices
2 teaspoons unsweetened cocoa powder
chunk of baking chocolate to shave for garnish
fresh lavender and mint sprigs for garnish

Slice strawberries, and set aside ½ cup strawberry slices.

In a large mixing bowl, beat cream cheese, powdered sugar, and pulverized lavender flowers until well blended. Fold in the whipped topping gradually until blended.

In a small bowl, mix coffee and coffee-flavored liqueur.

Line an 8-inch square baking dish with enough upside-down lady finger halves or pound cake slices to cover bottom of pan; if necessary trim lady fingers or pound cake to fit. Spoon ⅓ cup coffee mixture evenly over lady fingers or pound cake. Top with about a third of the cheese mixture, or about 1 cup. Layer half the remaining strawberries, about 1 cup, over the cheese mixture.

Repeat layers twice more, ending with cheese mixture.

Cover and refrigerate tiramisu and the reserved strawberries for at least an hour, up to 24 hours.

To serve, remove cover, sift cocoa powder over top. Arrange reserved strawberries over cocoa. Cut into squares, place on serving plates, and garnish with chocolate shavings and fresh lavender and mint sprigs. Makes 1 8-inch square pan.

Lavender Fruit Pizza with Lavender-Orange Glaze

This light, yummy dessert is perfect on a warm summer evening when fruits are plentiful. Choose the ones given in the recipe, or select your own combination. An especially nice combo for celebrating July 4th is strawberries, blueberries, and firm bananas.

1 18-ounce tube refrigerator sugar cookie dough
2 tablespoons dried lavender buds, pulverized with mortar and pestle, divided
2 8-ounce packages cream cheese, room temperature
1 tablespoon sugar
½ teaspoon vanilla extract
2 medium firm bananas, sliced
juice of 1 lemon
2½ cups fresh pineapple chunks, or canned pineapple chunks in their own juice
1 pint fresh strawberries, halved
2 kiwi fruit, peeled and sliced
½ pint fresh cherries, stemmed and pitted, or ½ cup red seedless grapes, or 1 small can mandarin oranges, drained
½ cup orange marmalade
3 tablespoons freshly squeezed orange juice
mint sprigs for garnish
fresh lavender sprigs for garnish

Preheat oven to 375º. Cut a circle of baking parchment to fit a 14-inch pizza pan or baking stone. Line pizza pan with parchment circle. If using a baking stone, preheat unlined stone in oven. With lightly oiled fingers, press the cookie dough to form a circle almost to the edge of the parchment; try to achieve a uniform thickness. Place pizza pan in oven, or if using a baking stone, transfer cookie dough on parchment to stone. Bake at 375º for 10–12 minutes, or until golden brown and fragrant. Remove from oven and let cool.

Pulverize dried lavender buds with mortar and pestle.

Combine cream cheese, sugar, 1 tablespoon pulverized lavender buds, and vanilla extract, mixing until smooth and evenly blended. Spread uniformly over baked, cooled cookie dough to within a quarter-inch of the edges.

Arrange the fruit in concentric circles, overlapping sliced fruit and abutting halves and chunks, starting with pineapple for the outside circle, followed by strawberries, bananas, kiwis, and cherries or grapes or mandarin oranges.

Combine the marmalade, orange juice, and remaining 1 tablespoon pulverized lavender buds, and mix until well blended. Heat in microwave oven for 60 seconds on medium. Sparingly spoon the mixture as a glaze over the fruit.

To serve, cut with a pizza cutter and place on dessert plates. Garnish with a sprig of mint and lavender. Serves 6–8.

Suzanne's Lavender Crunchies for Pets

Although the gourmet recipe is labeled as a dog recipe, my cat-owner friends say their cats like this treat as much as dogs, and both cats and dogs like the second recipe. Our Standard Schnauzer show dogs love these great treats for training and in the show ring.

Suzanne's Gourmet Lavender Dog Crunchies

1 ½ pounds chicken wings, backs, and liver, cooked and ground (bones included)
1 15-ounce can oil-packed salmon, mackerel, or tuna, chopped in the can
1 ½ cups rye flour
2 cups whole wheat flour
2 ½ cups brown rice flour
2 teaspoons garlic powder
4 tablespoons powdered kelp or other sea vegetable
4 tablespoons lavender buds, crumbled
1 ½ cups powdered milk
¾ cups brewer's yeast
5 tablespoons olive or rapeseed oil
1 cup goat's milk or sheep's milk
Reserved broth from boiling chicken, plus enough beef, chicken, or vegetable broth or stock to make 3 cups

Preheat oven to 350°. Lightly oil a large cookie sheet.
Cook chicken in enough water to cover; let cool. Remove chicken to grinder, reserving broth for later. Finely grind chicken parts, including bones. In a large bowl, stir together rye, whole wheat, and brown rice flours. Add garlic and kelp powders, crumbled lavender buds, powdered milk, and brewer's yeast. Mix in ground chicken, canned fish and its liquid to dry-ingredient mixture. Mix together olive oil, milk, and reserved broth plus stock; then blend into the mixture in the bowl. On a floured surface, roll out to ¼-inch thickness; cut into dogbone shapes with cookie cutter, or cut into squares appropriately sized for your dog(s). Place on oiled cookie sheet and bake at 350° until golden brown. Cool before giving any to your dog. Store in refrigerator in airtight container.

Suzanne's Lavender Pet Crunchies

1 ½ cups rye flour
1 ½ cups whole wheat flour
1 ½ cups brown rice flour
1 cup wheat germ
½ cup powdered milk
4 tablespoons dried lavender buds and leaves, crumbled
1 teaspoon dried kelp or other sea vegetable or alfalfa
1 teaspoon garlic powder
1/4 teaspoon ground ginger
1/2 teaspoon thyme leaves, crumbled
1 egg, beaten
4 tablespoons olive, rapeseed, or canola oil
1 ¼ cups beef, chicken, or vegetable broth or stock

Preheat oven to 350°. Lightly oil a large cookie sheet.
In a large bowl, stir together rye, whole wheat, and brown rice flours. Add wheat germ, powdered milk, crumbled lavender buds, kelp and garlic powders, ginger, and thyme. Beat the egg; mix in the oil and the broth or stock. Stir slowly into the dry-ingredient mixture. On a floured surface, roll out to ¼-inch thickness; cut into dogbone shapes with cookie cutter, or cut into squares appropriately sized for your dog(s). Place on oiled cookie sheet and bake at 350° until golden brown. Cool before giving any to your dog. Store in refrigerator in airtight container.

Bibliography

This is by no means a complete bibliography of all the books available that make reference to lavender—instead, it is simply those books in my personal library from which I drew much of the information for the introduction to this book. I hope my lavender cookbook inspires you to begin your own quest for information about this splendid herb.

Blose, Nora, and Dawn Cusick. *Herb Drying Handbook*. New York: Sterling/Lark, 1993.

Bottom Line Health, Editors of. *Uncommon Cures for Everyday Ailments*. Greenwich, CT: Bottom Line Books, 2000.

Boxer, Arabella, and Philippa Back. *The Herb Book*. London: Octopus Books Ltd., 1980.

Bremness, Lesley. *The Complete Book of Herbs: A practical guide to growing & using herbs*. New York: Viking Studio Books, 1988.

Dobelis, Inge N., Ed. *Magic and Medicine of Plants*. Pleasantville, NY: The Reader's Digest Association, 1986.

Freeman, Sally. *Herbs for All Seasons: Growing and Gathering Herbs for Flavor, Health and Beauty*. New York: Penguin, 1991.

Harrar, Sari, and Sara Altshul O'Donnell. *The Woman's Book of Healing Herbs: Secrets from 90 Top Herbalists*. Emmaus, PA: Rodale Books, 1999.

Hayes, Elizabeth S. *Spices and Herbs: Lore and Cookery*. New York: Dover Publications, 1961.

Herbst, Sharon Tyler. *Food Lover's Companion*. New York: Barron's Educational Series, Inc., 2001.

Kowalchik, Claire, and William H. Hylton, Eds. *Rodale's Illustrated Encyclopedia of Herbs*. Emmaus PA: Rodale Press, 1987.

Labensky, Sarah R., and Alan M. Hause. *On Cooking: Techniques from Expert Chefs*, 2nd Ed. Upper Saddle River, NJ: Prentice–Hall, 1995.

Labensky, Stephen, Gaye G. Ingram, and Sarah R. Labensky. *Webster's New World Dictionary of Culinary Arts*, 2nd Ed. Upper Saddle River, NJ: Prentice–Hall, 2001.

Lathrop, Norma Jean. *Herbs: How to Select, Grow, and Enjoy*. Tucson: HP Books, 1981.

Mabey, Richard, Michael McIntyre, Pamela Michael, Gail Duff, and John Stevens. *The New Age Herbalist*. New York: Collier Books, 1988.

McNair, Jane K., et al. *The World of Herbs and Spices*. Berkeley, CA: Ortho Books, 1978.

Miloradovich, Milo. *Growing and Using Herbs and Spices*. New York: Dover Books, 1986.

Ogden, Shepherd, and Ellen Ogden. *The Cook's Garden: Growing and Using the Best-tasting Vegetable Varieties*. Emmaus, PA: Rodale Press, 1989.

Phillips, Roger, and Nicky Foy. *The Random House Book of Herbs*. New York: Random House, 1990.

Potterton, David, Ed. *Culpepper's Color Herbal*. New York: Sterling Publishing Co., 1983 (*Culpepper's Herbal* originally published in 1649).

Root, Waverly, Ed. *Herbs and Spices: A Guide to Culinary Seasoning*, New and Revised Edition. New York: Alfred van der Marck Editions, 1985.

Rose, Jeanne. *Jeanne Rose's Herbal Guide to Food*. Berkeley, CA: North Atlantic Books, 1979.

Shaudys, Phyllis. *The Pleasure of Herbs: A Month-by-Month Guide to Growing, Using, and Enjoying Herbs*. Pownal, VT: Storey Communications, Inc., 1986.

Weiner, Michael A.. and Janet A. Weiner. *Herbs that Heal*. Mill Valley, CA: Quantum Books, 1994.

Index

Meats 18-22
   Greek Lamb Chops with Lavender 19
   Grilled Lamb Chops with Herbes de Provence 18
   Grilled Marinated Filets Mignons on Lavender Foil Bread 20
   Lavender-laced Filets Mignons 21
   Sautéed Veal Scallops with Lavender-Lemon Sauce 22
Other 49
   Suzanne's Lavender Crunchies for Pets 49
Pasta 23
   Pasta with Fresh Herbs 23
Poultry 17, 23, 47
   Lavender Chicken with Rosemary and Lemon 17
   Pasta with Fresh Herbs 23
   Lavender and Buttermilk Fried Chicken 47
Salads 11, 46
   Lavender-Scented Crabmeat Mousse 11
   Lavender Watermelon Salad 46
Soups 9, 10
   Red Raspberry-Lavender Soup 9
   Wild Mushroom-Barley Soup with Lavender 10
Vegetables 24-28
   Lavender Peas 27
   Lavender Fried Apples 25
   Mediterranean Carrots 26
   New Potatoes with Lemon-Lavender-Chive Butter 24
   Zucchini Provençal 28

About the Author

Suzanne Smith is a former research scientist who has been writing stories, poems, and nonfiction since she was five years old. She is the author of four previous books, *Pumpkin Recipes*—a collection of exciting recipes using the humble pumpkin; *Recipes for Romance*—a compilation of recipes for every stage of courtship, including the time when your nest is empty and you're re-kindling your romance; *The Standard Schnauzer in America: Sourcebook II*; and *Handbook for the International Information Economy*. A member of New Mexico Book Association, Southwest Writers, Romance Writers of America and two of its chapters, and Los Alamos Writers Group, she teaches writing classes at the University of New Mexico at Los Alamos and is hard at work on several new fiction and nonfiction writing projects. In her spare time, she grows orchids and herbs, tends her roses, teaches piano to adults, gives an occasional piano concert, and romps with her dogs, who grudgingly consent to be exhibited at random dog shows. She invented some of the recipes in this book and collected others from friends, family, and colleagues in her travels around the world with her husband, Ron, who indulges her in all her obsessions du jour.

CPSIA information can be obtained at www.ICGtesting.com
Printed in the USA
BVOW010502100713

325492BV00008BB/178/P